ALLAH

AR-RAHMAAN

The Most or Entirely Merciful

AR-RAHEEM

The Bestower of Mercy

AL-MALIK

The Eternal Lord

AL-QUDDUS

The Most Sacred

AS-SALAM

The embodiment of Peace

ASOKLAM

The Embodiment of Peace

AL-MU'MIN

The Infuser of Faith

AL-MUHAYMIN

The Guardian, The Overseer

AL-AZEEZ

The All Mighty

AL-JABBAR

The Compeller

AL-MUTAKABBIR

The Supreme, The Majestic

AL-KHAALIQ

The Creator

AL-BAARI'

The Originator

AL-MUSAWWIR

The Fashioner

AL-GHAFFAR

The Great Forgiver

AL-QAHHAR

The Subduer

AL-GAHHAR

AL-WAHHAAB

The Supreme Bestower

AR-RAZZAAQ

The Provider

AL-FATTAAH

The Supreme Solver

AL-'ALEEM

The All-Knowing

AL-'ALEEM

The All-Knowing

AL-QAABID

The Withholder

AL-BAASIT

The Extender

AL-KHAAFIDH

The Reducer

AR-RAAFI'

The Exalter, The Elevator

AL-MU'IZZ

The Honourer

AL-MUZIL

The Humiliator

AS-SAMEE'

The All-Hearing

AL-BASEER

The All-Seeing

AL-HAKAM

The Impartial Judge

AL-'ADL

The Utterly Just

AL-LATEEF

The Most Gentle

AL-KHABEER

The All-Aware

AL-HALEEM

The Most Forbearing

AL-'ATHEEM

The Supreme

AL-GHAFOOR

The Forgiving

ASH-SHAKOOR

The Most Appreciative

AL-'ALEE

The Most High, The Exalted

AL-KABEER

The Greatest

AL-HAFEEDH

The Preserver

AL-MUQEET

The Sustainer

AL-HASEEB

The Reckoner, The Sufficient

AL-JALEEL

The Majestic

VALLÉE

The Majestic

AL-KAREEM

The Most Generous

AR-RAQEEB

The Watchful

AL-MUJEEB

The Responsive One

AL-WAASI'

The All-Encompassing

AL-HAKEEM

The All-Wise

AL-HAKEEM

The All-Wise

AL-WADOOD

The Most Loving

AL-MAJEED

The Glorious

AL-BA'ITH

The Infuser of New Life

ASH-SHAHEED

The All- and Ever Witnessin

AL-HAQQ

The Absolute Truth

AL-WAKEEL

The Trustee

AL-QAWIYY

The All-Strong

AL-MATEEN

The Firm

AL-WALIYY

The Protecting Associate

AL-HAMEED

The Praiseworthy

AL-MUHSEE

The All-Enumerating

AL-MUBDI

The Initiator

AL-MU'ID

The Restorer, The Reinstater

AL-MUHYEE

The Giver of Life

AL-MUMEET

The Bringer of Death

AL-HAYY

The Ever-Living

AL-QAYYOOM

The Self-Subsisting

AL-WAAJID

The Perceiver

AL-MAAJID

The Illustrious, the Magnificent

AL-WAAHID

The one

AL-AHAD

The Unique

AS-SAMAD

The Eternal, Satisfier of Needs

AL-QADIR

The Capable

AL-MUQTADIR

The Omnipotent

AL-MUQADDIM

The Expediter

AL-MU'AKHKHIR

The Delayer

AL-AWWAL

The First

AL-AAKHIR

The last

AZ-DHAAHIR

The Manifest

AL-BAATIN

The Hidden One

AL-WALLI

The Governor , The Patron

AL-MUTA'ALI

The Self Exalted

AL-BARR

The Source of Goodness

AT-TAWWAB

The Ever-Pardoning

AL-MUNTAQIM

The Avenger

AL-'AFUWW

The Pardoner

AR-RA'OOF

The Most Kind

MAALIK-UL-MULK

Master of the Kingdom

DHUL-JALAALI WAL-IKRAAM

Lord of Majesty and Generosity

AL-MUQSIT

The Equitable

AL-JAAMI'

TThe Gatherer, the Uniter

AL-GHANIYY

The Self-Sufficient, The Wealthy

AL-MUGHNI

The Enricher

AL-MANI'

The Withholder

AL-WAHHAB

The Withholder

AL-DHARR

The Distresser

AN-NAFI'

The Propitious, the Benefactor

AN-NUR

The Light, The Illuminator

AL-HAADI

The Guide

AL-BADEE'

TThe Incomparable Originator

AL-BAAQI

The Ever-Surviving

AL-WAARITH

The Inheritor, The Heir

AR-RASHEED

The Guide, Infallible Teacher

AS-SABOOR

The Forbearing, The Patient